Our Money

Towards a new monetary system

Our Money – Towards a New Monetary System

First edition

© 2015 Frans Doorman. All rights reserved.

ISBN: 978-1-329-08349-3

This work is licensed under the Creative Commons Attribution-NonCommercial-NoDerivs 2.0. To view a copy of this license, visit http://creativecommons.org/licenses/by-nc-nd/3.0/

Keywords: money, monetary system, financial system, money creation, economic crisis, financial crisis, private money creation, banks, public money creation, sustainable development

Published through Lulu internet publishers: www.lulu.com

Our Money

Towards a new monetary system

Frans Doorman

Commercial banks create checkbook money whenever they grant a loan, simply by adding new deposit dollars in accounts on their books in exchange for a borrower's IOU. Federal Reserve Bank of New York; Friedman, David H. (1977). *I Bet You Thought....*, p. 19. OCLC 5356154.

Whenever a bank makes a loan, it simultaneously creates a matching deposit in the borrower's bank account, thereby creating new money. Bank of England (2014), *Money creation in the modern economy.* http://www.bankofengland.co.uk/publications/Documents/quarterlybulletin/2014/qb14q102.pdf.

The process by which banks create money is so simple that the mind is repelled. John Kenneth Galbraith, *Money: Whence it came, Where it Went* (1975), p. 29.

The study of money, above all other fields in economics, is one in which complexity is used to disguise truth or to evade truth, not to reveal it. John Kenneth Galbraith, *Money: Whence it came, where it went* (1975), p. 15.

ACKNOWLEDGEMENTS

"Our Money", "Ons Geld" in Dutch, is a Dutch foundation aiming for monetary reform by having the state take responsiblity for money creation. With thanks to Martijn-Jeroen van der Linden, Lou Keune, Roelf Haan, Socrates Schouten and Luuk de Waal Malefijt for their comments and suggestions, which improved the original Dutch version of this booklet considerably. All remaining errors and other shortcomings are, of course, my responsibility.

TABLE OF CONTENTS

ACKNOWLEDGEMENTS 4
TABLE OF CONTENTS 5
PREFACE: ABOUT THIS BOOKLET 9
SUMMARY 11

1.   LACK OF MONEY 15
    PROBLEMS: ECONOMIC, SOCIAL, ENVIRONMENTAL 15
    LACK OF MONEY 15
    CREATING MONEY 16
    UNDERSTANDING OUR MONETARY SYSTEM 16
    QUESTIONS WE SHOULD ASK 17

2.   WHAT IS MONEY? 19
    WHAT IS MONEY? 19
    MONEY AS A MEDIUM OF EXCHANGE AND UNIT OF ACCOUNT 19
    MONEY AS A MEANS FOR ACCUMULATION OR SAVING 19
    THE FOUNDATION OF MONEY: TRUST 20

3.   WHAT HAVE WE MADE OF MONEY? 21
    MONEY AS MAGIC 21
    THE GREATEST FEAR: (HYPER) INFLATION 21
    MONEY SCARCITY AND ECONOMIC THEORY 21
    WHY GOVERNMENTS DON'T CREATE MONEY 22
    MONEY, ECONOMIC THEORY AND SPECULATION 22
    DISCUSSING OUR MONETARY SYSTEM: EXPERTS ONLY 23
    THE COMPARISON WITH NUCLEAR ENERGY 23
    OUR MONETARY SYSTEM AS A GIVEN 24
    MONEY AS A SCARCE RESOURCE 24
    SOMETHING FOR NOTHING? 25

4.   HOW IS MONEY CREATED? 27
    HOW MONEY IS CREATED 27
    BANKING: GOOD BUSINESS 27

5.   WHY MONEY CREATION BY PRIVATE BANKS? 29
    A LEGACY OF HISTORY 29
    AN EFFECTIVE LOBBY 29
    A MATTER OF TRUST 30

6. DRAWBACKS OF OUR SYSTEM 31

PRIVATE MONEY CREATION: FROM CRISIS TO CRISIS 31
ECONOMIC THEORY: FINANCIAL MARKETS CANNOT WORK 31
PRIVATE BANKS: A BRAKE ON MONEY CREATION? 32
MONEY TO THE FINANCIAL ECONOMY 33
BANKING: SOCIALISM FOR THE RICH 34
PRIVATE MONEY CREATION: UPS AND DOWNS 35
A SMALL GROUP BENEFITS FROM BANKING 35
BANK BELLY UP, MONEY GONE 36
CREDIT, INTEREST RATE AND DEBT 36
DEBT LEADS TO A GROWTH IMPERATIVE 37
THE GROWTH IMPERATIVE AND FINITE RESOURCES 37
OUR MONETARY SYSTEM AND FINITE RESOURCES 38
MONEY CREATION ONLY FOR PROFITABLE ACTIVITIES 38
GOVERNMENT AS A PARASITIC ENTITY 39
FOSTERING POVERTY AND IMPOVERISHMENT 39
ADVANTAGES OF PRIVATE MONEY CREATION? 39
THE DEFENCE OF THE PRESENT SYSTEM 40

7. HOW CAN WE DO BETTER? 43

THE ALTERNATIVE: PUBLIC MONEY CREATION 43
PUBLIC OR PRIVATE BANKING? 44
ADVANTAGES OF PUBLIC MONEY CREATION 44
AN END TO THE GROWTH IMPERATIVE 46
A MORE STABLE ECONOMY 46
LESS SPECULATION, NO MORE BAIL-OUTS 46
FEWER RISKS, SAVINGS SAFE 47
TRANSPARENCY 48
RISKS OF PUBLIC MONEY CREATION 48
PREVENTING DEMAND AND COST INFLATION 49
TRANSITION 50
MANDATE OF THE MONETARY AUTHORITY 51
CHANNELLING NEW MONEY INTO THE ECONOMY 51

8. OBSTACLES AND SOLUTIONS 53

INFLATION PHOBIA 53
PRIVATE MONEY CREATION AS ECONOMIC DOGMA 54
THE REAL CAUSE OF INFLATION 54
MAINTAINING CONFIDENCE 55
CAN THE TRANSITION BE MADE IN ONE COUNTRY? 55
PSYCHOLOGICAL OBSTACLES 57

OVERCOMING PSYCHOLOGICAL BARRIERS 57
INFLUENCE OF THE BANKS: MONEY IS POWER 58
ECONOMIC DOGMA PROTECTS FINANCIAL SYSTEM AND BANKS 59
BREAKING THE POWER OF THE FINANCIAL SECTOR 60
OUR BIGGEST MISTAKE: DELEGATION 62

9. WHAT TO DO? 65

OPENING THE DEBATE 65
DISCUSSION BASED ON ARGUMENTS 65
AN UPHILL BATTLE 66
MONEY ISN'T DIFFICULT 66
TARGET GROUP: OUR POLITICIANS 67
THE TRANSITION: PLANNING AHEAD 67
A ROLE FOR ECONOMISTS? 68

POSTSCRIPT: MONEY CREATION AND SUSTAINABLE DEVELOPMENT 71

MONEY FOR SUSTAINABLE DEVELOPMENT: A POLITICAL CHOICE 71
MONEY CREATION AND NON-SUSTAINABLE CONSUMPTION 72
AN INTEGRATED APPROACH 73
TRANSITION TO SUSTAINABLE: WITH OR WITHOUT GROWTH? 74
FIRST GROWTH, THEN STEADY STATE 74
GROWTH FOR SUSTAINABLE DEVELOPMENT 75

ANNEX: NETWORKS, READING, VIEWING 77

ORGANISATIONS 77
VIDEOS 78
BOOKS AND REPORTS 79
MORE TECHNICAL PUBLICATIONS 83

Our Money – Towards a New Monetary System

PREFACE: ABOUT THIS BOOKLET

There are many misconceptions about money and our monetary system. Most people consider both as a fact of life, a kind of natural phenomenon that should be accepted as is. In other words, money and the monetary system are not seen, even by experts, as something that is human-made and therefore, in principle, something that can be changed as we see fit. Yet it can be changed: as a society we can make new agreements about money and organize our monetary system in a different way. Why we should do so is one of the things explained in this booklet.

Even specialists such as economists and bankers often provide a faulty explanation of what money is and how it is created. That's not really surprising: the Bank of England recently stated that explanations in many economic textbooks are also misconceived. In this book we'll try to explain, in plain English, what money is and how our current monetary system came about. We'll then discuss the problems inherent to the present system and propose an alternative.

This booklet also explains how the current monetary system restrains us in addressing our economic, social and environmental problems, and even worsens them. It discusses the transition to a system that would work better, the main traits of that system, and the reasons why such a better alternative is hardly considered at present.

This booklet is intended for a broad audience: anyone with an interest in the solution of society's social, environmental and economic challenges. People who are concerned about the continuing impact of the economic crisis that started in 2008 and about its aftermath: growing economic insecurity, inequality, and poverty. And people who are distressed about the environmental problems our global society is facing: the degradation of ecosystems and the environment in general, the depletion of natural resources, climate change, loss of agricultural land, and looming fresh water shortages. People who, even though they do not expect to be affected by these problems directly themselves are concerned about the future of their children and in general, of future generations.

That's a broad audience and the question can be raised what environmental problems have to do with our monetary system. That will be explained in this booklet, but it comes down to this. The knowledge and technology exist to address the challenges our society faces, certainly the environmental ones. The productive capacity to do so exists or can be developed relatively quickly. The prime reason too little is being done is that there's not enough money. And that, as we shall see, is the result of our current monetary system.

Organizations working on monetary reform exist in many countries. The movement is most developed in Britain and the United States, with Positive Money and The American Monetary Institute having elaborated full proposals for Parliament. In The Netherlands a so-called citizen's initiative to put money creation on the agenda of Parliament got 40,000 signatures within days and passed the 100,000 mark within two months.

The campaign to change the monetary system is not new. The Chicago Plan, a concept for a different monetary system comparable to that outlined in this booklet, almost made it into law in the United States in the 1930s.[1] Today's leading financial organization, the International Monetary Fund (IMF), recently published a report in which the Chicago Plan is discussed and its effects on the economy modelled, with very positive conclusions.[2]

Yet there is a long way to go before the current monetary system and the discussion about alternatives will be firmly on the mainstream political and public agenda. This booklet aims to contribute to getting it there. Not only to cope with the problems and injustices resulting from the current system but also, and especially so, because change of the system is crucial to addressing the economic, social and environmental challenges facing our society.

---

[1] The bankers lobby managed to block implementation of the Plan by the Roosevelt administration, in spite of the fact that is was actively supported by many prominent economists and other academics.

[2] *The Chicago Plan Revisited*, J. Benes & M. Kumhof, 2012, IMF Working Paper, http://www.imf.org/external/pubs/ft/wp/2012/wp12202.pdf

SUMMARY

The main arguments in this booklet can be summarized as follows:

1) **Our current monetary system blocks both the tackling of the social and environmental problems society faces and a way out of the crisis**

The technological knowledge, labour and productive capacity to address society's problems exist or can be developed soon. The fact that our resources are not used to do so is a direct result of the current monetary system, which leads to money being created and used for other ends. Thus our monetary system blocks tackling the main problems society faces as well as a way out of the crisis.

2) **Money need not be scarce**

Money is a medium of exchange, unit of account and means of saving. It is something artificial on which we have agreed as representing a certain value. Because most money is electronic, meaning it does not physically exist but only occurs in the memory banks of computers, it can, in principle, be created at will.

3) **Money as an obstacle to tackling society's problems**

We are told that the major problem in addressing society's environmental, social and economic problems is lack of money. That is irrational: since money can, in principle, be made at will the lack of it should never be an obstacle to addressing society's challenges.

4) **Money creation: the privilege of private banks**

Almost all of our money is created by private banks. It is created out of thin air by an accounting practice engaged in when a bank makes a loan. The privilege of being able to create money in this manner endows banks with profits that should benefit society as a whole.

5) **The current system leads to instability and indebtedness**

The current system of money creation leads to instability and crisis. Private banks create too much money when things go well and too little when the economy is doing poorly needs it. Private money creation is inextricably linked to interest, leading to mounting debts which may become impossible to repay after a slump.

6) No money for solving society's problems and investments in sustainable development

Money is created only for what banks and their customers find important, not for the public good. For the latter the government must raise money, through taxes or borrowing. As a result of existing government obligations and debt, worsened by bailing out banks during the financial crisis, there is too little money for investment for the public interest.

7) Disadvantages of money creation by private banks: from crisis to crisis

Irresponsible lending by private banks caused the financial crisis of 2008. Since then central banks have tried to address the economic crisis by encouraging banks to lend more to the "real" economy of goods and services. In practice much of this money is used for speculation, of which private banks and other financial players expect higher returns. Thus private banks, supported by central banks, are laying the basis for the next crisis.

8) Public money creation

Governments have little control over money creation and distribution. This lack of control over a key resource is a democratic deficit at the expense of the public interest. Money creation is a public service which should be under the control of the state. Public money creation by an independent monetary authority is a logical and attractive alternative to money creation by private banks. Such a system would allow bringing new money into the economy without creating debt.

9) Benefits of public money creation

Public money creation would reduce both public and private debt. It would curb economic ups and downs, speculation and thus the risk of financial crisis. It would give more options to fight inflation and deflation. And it would give the state much ampler resources for investment, without requiring higher taxes or debt.

10) Public money creation can remedy the addiction to growth

Public money creation would eliminate the need for economic growth, a requisite arising from the fact that with private money creation debts have to be repaid with interest. With government creating debt-free money this imperative disappears, opening the way for an economy and society using finite resources in a sustainable manner.

11) Money creation for solving society's problems: a political choice

Public money creation would give government greater leeway for investment in the public interest. However, politicians and voters must opt for such spending: the benefits of public money creation can also be used for (more) unsustainable consumption and thereby the faster exhaustion of finite resources.

12) Faith in markets impedes the search for alternatives

A major obstacle to monetary reform is mainstream economic science. The belief that market forces will ensure that banks create the right amount of money for an optimally functioning economy leads to the current monetary system not even being questioned. So strong is this belief in markets that even the enormous problems caused by the crisis of 2008 have given economists no cause to look for alternatives.

13) The need to open the debate on an alternative financial system

A debate about the current monetary system and the alternative, public money creation, is urgently needed. Political parties but also civil society organizations such as trade unions, environmental groups and other voluntary, non-profit and interest groups should pressure their political representatives to open this debate.

1. LACK OF MONEY

Problems: economic, social, environmental

The past hundred years have brought us unprecedented development, especially through ever-evolving technology. In consequence never in history have so many people have lived so well. Yet our society and humanity as a whole are facing huge problems. Since the 1980s lower and middle incomes have barely risen, despite the fact that technology and productivity have continued to develop. The benefits of this development are going mostly to corporations and to the highest income groups, leading to an increasingly large and still growing gap between rich and poor. Especially after the 2008 crisis persistent unemployment and declining livelihoods are leading to impoverishment, with major social and psychological consequences. On top of that people are faced with higher costs of and decreased access to public services such as health care and education.

In addition to these economic and social problems there are enormous environmental challenges: climate change, the depletion of natural resources, the destruction of nature, pollution, growing water shortages, the loss of agricultural land. Problems which are already making an impact, especially in the form of extreme weather, but which will hit much harder in the longer term. In order to prevent this we have to start addressing them as soon as possible.

Lack of money

A key element in the failure to address these problems is money. Ask our politicians to effectively address climate change: no money. Investing in energy efficiency and renewable energy: no money. Nature and environment: no money. But also: better and cheaper education: no money. Employment programs: no money. In other words, there is, at least at this time, no money for those things that are important to the quality of life for present and future generations, such as good public services, a clean environment and the responsible use of natural resources.

Creating money

All things considered it is strange that we do not address such important problems due to lack of money. After all, money can, in principle, be created at will. Most money is electronic: it does not even exist physically. Tangible money, coins and banknotes, form only two to three percent of the total money supply. The remaining 97 percent goes under various names: deposit money, bank money, scriptural money and more recently, electronic money: it exists only in the memory banks of computers. Of that we can create as much as we need: all it takes is a few keystrokes on the right computer.

In practice there are limitations to creating money, such as the quantity of goods and services the economy can produce. But if, as has been the case after the 2008 crisis, production is much below that capacity it would appear logical to create money to garner the underused capacity of our economy to address society's challenges. Doing so would have the additional advantage of triggering the private sector investment and job creation that would help overcome the economic crisis.

It doesn't happen. Production capacity remains unused, problems are insufficiently addressed, and the crisis continues. Companies go bankrupt, unemployment remains high. The explanation for this lies with the way money is created presently, with the current monetary system.

Understanding our monetary system

The concept of money and the way our monetary system works are not well understood. This applies not only to the average citizen: even specialists, such as economists and bankers, often have a false image. That's understandable to some extent, considering the comment of the British central bank, the Bank of England, that many economic textbooks give a false image of how money is created.[3]

---

[3]

http://www.bankofengland.co.uk/publications/Documents/quarterlybulletin/2014/qb14q102.pdf

Without some insight into how the current monetary system works a discussion about whether and how we should improve the system is difficult. Therefore this booklet tries to explain in as simple a manner as possible how the current monetary system works, how it originated, what's wrong with it, and what should be done about it.

Questions we should ask

The starting point for our explanation consists of two questions – with brief introductions. First: our society is facing huge environmental and social problems that threaten the welfare of billions of people, now and even more so in the future. The main reason these problems are not addressed on the required scale is lack of money. The question is: how is it that lack of money, the only resource that can be created at will, forms the main obstacle for addressing effectively society's problems?

The second question is: what can we do about it? How can we ensure that lack of money is no longer an obstacle to tackling these problems? It is these two questions this booklet aims to answer.

Our Money – Towards a New Monetary System

2. WHAT IS MONEY?

What is money?

Money is a medium of exchange, unit of account and means of saving. As a medium of exchange money serves to facilitate trade. As such it works if people accept it as something that represents a certain value. It is something artificial, something of which we tacitly assume as having and keeping that certain value.

Money as a medium of exchange and unit of account

In the absence of money goods and services have to be bartered: someone who has too much of a product, say sugar, and needs another product, say salt, must find someone who has salt *and* is interested in exchanging it for sugar. Money, in the form of coins, bills, or in some societies, shells or cattle, makes it possible for the person having sugar to sell it even if the buyer has no salt. The seller then looks for someone who wants to sell salt. This is a lot easier than finding a person with both properties: a need for sugar and salt to sell. Money is something so practical that through the centuries it was "invented" in all but the simplest societies. Because money ensures a much more flexible process of exchange it is the lubricant of the economy.

Added to the use of money as a unit of exchange is its function as a unit of account. Because of this feature, it is possible to compare the value of different products or services with each other.

Money as a means for accumulation or saving

A third function of money is that you can accumulate and hoard it, so as to use it at a later point in time. Money takes up very little space (except the cattle) and does not spoil. Accumulation leads to trade in money: those who need it but do not have it can borrow money from someone who has money to spare. The loan is paid back later, usually with interest: a premium that makes lending money attractive. Lending is also done by intermediaries: people taking savings from others and lending them to third parties. That's how banking began.

The foundation of money: trust

The foundation on which the value of money is built is trust. For money to fulfil its role as a means of exchange and accumulation people must believe two things. The first is that it will be accepted widely as payment; the second, related one is that it will keep its value. If this confidence is lost money will loose its value as a medium of exchange, as a means of accumulation and as a unit of account.

3. WHAT HAVE WE MADE OF MONEY?

Money as magic

The principle of money is very simple. But especially during the past two centuries money has taken on an almost magical character. It is no longer seen as something created by man that, therefore, can be manipulated freely, but as something that conforms to its own laws that are beyond the control of mere humans. Therefore we barely dare intervene in the monetary system: we are afraid this will lead to uncontrollable events determined by timeless monetary laws, with terrible financial and economic consequences.

The greatest fear: (hyper) inflation

The greatest fear is for hyperinflation: money rapidly losing its value with fatal consequences for the monetary system and the economy as a whole. This fear is greatest in people with a lot of money, but ordinary people with some savings and employees whose salaries are not automatically adjusted to inflation also suffer heavily. Only those with large debts benefit: their debts are all but wiped out as the value of money approaches zero.

Money scarcity and economic theory

The science responsible for assigning magical properties to money is economics. Mainstream economic theory assumes that economic systems are in balance or are moving towards a balance, or with a fancy word, equilibrium. So too with money: economists assume that the money supply is balanced with supply and demand. Therefore, in line with general economic theory, the quantity theory of money teaches that pumping more money into the economy without a corresponding increase in the production of goods and services inflation, meaning an increase in the overall price level, is inevitable. This theory has never been proven, is – as we'll see later – refuted by the facts. It is, in fact, little more than faith, based on a series of assumptions that have little to do with reality. But as a faith it is so dominant among economists and in their wake policy makers, politicians, the media, and almost anyone who thinks he or she knows something about economics that it's at the basis of all financial policy.

Why governments don't create money

The money supply theory explains why governments do not create money for their own use. It is fear: the fear of money creation by government causing uncontrollable inflation.[4] This fear of inflation is so strong that money creation by the government for use by the government has become a taboo. The only safe way to create money, so it's assumed, is to subject it to market forces. This means money creation should be left to the private sector: to banks operating in a competitive market. Market forces will ensure that the quantity of money stays in balance with on the one hand, the quantity of goods and services and on the other, demand for those goods and services. Anything occurring outside the market, such as a government creating money (through the central bank) for its own use will, it is strongly believed, upset the balance established by the market and, in line with the quantity theory of money, cause inflation.

Money, economic theory and speculation

Over the years economists have developed all kinds of complex theories about money. Intricate mathematical models and equations have needlessly complicated the concept of money and especially, the way money works in our monetary and economic system. Since the 1990s such models have been used in financial markets for speculation: trying to make money by trading in money and financial products. Trillions of dollars are involved, as a result of which financial businesses hire the smartest economists and mathematicians in the hope their models will do the best job in predicting the market and thereby, maximizing profits. The models and financial products they produce have become so complicated that they are only understood by the very best minds. Even the supervisory boards and boards of directors of the financial institutions employing these geniuses often do not understand the

---

[4] Inflation of one or two percent is generally considered acceptable and even preferable. If inflation rises above 4% it's seen as a (serious) problem.

exact nature of the financial products involved and their effects on the economy.

Discussing our monetary system: experts only

The biggest problem with this complexity is that non-economists do not dare speak out about our monetary system. Only the experts have their say – and despite the mess caused by the 2008 crisis, foreseen by practically none[5], they continue venting their opinions with such aplomb that laymen will think twice about calling their expertise into question. Thus the thinking about what we would like our monetary system to be remains the exclusive reserve of a small group of insiders.

The comparison with nuclear energy

We should approach our monetary system as we do nuclear energy. We don't have much of a clue of the workings of a nuclear power plant: that's all enormously complicated technology – just as all those mathematical models depicting our economy are terribly complicated. But we do form an opinion on whether we want nuclear power or not. We are smart enough to weigh the pros and cons of nuclear energy when properly informed. And, after comparison with alternative forms of energy generation, we can express our opinion on whether we want such energy or not. Thus many people have formed an opinion about nuclear energy. Those who have not will usually say that they do not know enough of the pros, cons and alternatives.

Our monetary system as a given

What applies to nuclear power should also apply to our monetary system. At present almost everyone assumes that the system is a

---

[5] Some experts did foresee the crisis – some economists and more often, non-economists who observed the facts and used logical reasoning to predict that pre-crisis events would lead to a financial melt-down. No model and therefore, no economists basing themselves on their models foresaw the impending disaster.

given, that there are no alternatives, and that therefore we have no choice but to continue with it – perhaps with some of the minor adjustments proposed by experts. This attitude must change. We can and, in our own interest and that of future generations, should form an opinion on the current system, look at the advantages and disadvantages, and explore alternatives. And we must take action to get a better alternative introduced. As in the case of nuclear power we should not be discouraged by the fact that we do not exactly or even approximately understand how the current system works. Important are the actual and likely outcomes of the current system, and those of alternative systems.

Money as a scarce resource

In analyzing the current monetary system and its alternatives we should let go of ingrained ideas, especially the assumption that money is scarce. This assumption has taken hold under the influence of mainstream economics. Economists and other financial experts believe the amount of money is limited, and that society will have to live with the limitations imposed by that scarcity.

If indeed there is scarcity, a lack of money, it is self-imposed since as mentioned, in principle money can be created at will. The problem is that current attitudes and outlook make this idea difficult to accept. The idea that money can be made out of nothing runs against our deepest beliefs. Something for nothing, a free lunch, impossible - money has to be earned! The idea that we could just make money to, for example, repay a portion of the national debt or invest in renewable energy generation, energy conservation and better roads is hard to acknowledge. There must be a snag somewhere, a fly in the ointment. And yet it can be done: as mentioned, we do not even have to produce the money physically, in the form of banknotes or coins. As most money is electronic a few keystrokes on the right keyboard would suffice.

Something for nothing?

What we have to remember when we talk about money and the "there is no such thing as a free lunch" argument comes up is that actually, money *is* nothing. As said, most of it does not even exist physically, and even if it does, in the form of coins or paper money, it has almost no intrinsic value. You can't do anything useful with coins or banknotes: you can't eat, sleep, live, or move in them. Money, then, is nothing more than a symbol. Symbols you can create freely, especially if they are electronic. And because symbols are nothing you get, if you create money, not something for nothing, but nothing for nothing.

That does not mean there are no restrictions on money creation. The limitation, however, is not in the money itself, but in the products you buy for it: a meal or the ingredients for it, a bed, a house, a bicycle. Of these there are limited quantities. Therefore, the fact that in principle we can make unlimited amounts of money does not mean we should. We should not create so much money that producers can ask much higher prices because their products are bought anyway, or that workers can demand much higher wages because they will be paid anyway. That would lead to an increase in the overall price level: the very definition of inflation. A low level of inflation is considered acceptable and, in the eyes of most economists, even desirable[6]. In most countries, therefore, central banks aim for inflation rates of about two percent, as this is considered to contribute to stimulate the economy and thereby, economic growth. But higher inflation is rightly seen as harmful to the economy, especially for those with savings and for employees.

---

[6] The reasoning is that a little inflation will encourage people and companies to consume and invest rather than save, because in the longer run the money will be worth less. Investment and consumption are good for the economy: money should be spent, not hoarded. Conversely economists argue that deflation, the lowering of the price level and thereby, increase of the value of money, will stimulate businesses and people to hoard their money because they assume it will further increase in value. This is bad for the economy: money not spent will reduce economic activity and thereby economic growth. It has never been proven that these arguments apply in reality, i.e., that people will actually postpone expenditure because they think money will be worth more in the future, but the belief in such "rational economic behaviour" is so strong that it has become established wisdom.

And it can, if it gets out of hand, lead to hyperinflation and a financial and economic crisis.

4. HOW IS MONEY CREATED?

How money is created

Most people, including many economists, think that central banks and thus government creates our money. The central bank then lends the money to ordinary banks, which bring it into the economy by lending to consumers, businesses and governments. People also believe that, apart from central bank money, the deposits in the (savings) accounts held by bank customers are an important source of the money lent by banks.

The idea that banks work only with money created by central banks and with the money depositors put in their care is wrong. In reality only about three percent of the total money supply, the part consisting of coins and banknotes, is created by the central bank. The remaining 97 percent of money is produced by private banks when they give loans. This is done through a simple accounting practice which results in the amount of the loan – and the money thus created – being added to both sides of the bank's balance sheet (for accountants among us: to the assets as a loan; to the liabilities as a deposit in the account of the borrower). As the British Central Bank, the Bank of England, put it in 2014: *"Whenever a bank makes a loan, it simultaneously creates a matching deposit in the borrower's bank account, thereby creating new money."*[7]

In theory the money created by lending is destroyed when the loan is repaid. In practice that does happen, but at the same time the amount of newly given credit is almost always much higher than the amount of credit repaid. Thus the money supply continues to increase.

Banking: good business

For private banks money creation is a lucrative business. Think about it: without having to produce anything tangible a product is created that can be marketed for a return - the interest on the loan -

---

[7] Bank of England (2014), Money creation in the modern economy, http://www.bankofengland.co.uk/publications/Documents/quarterlybulletin/2014/qb14q102.pdf.

of between 5% (mortgage) and as high as 15% (consumer credit). Of course some time and brainpower is spent on the assessment and administration of credit applications. But overall there is no trade in which it is so easy to make money - both literally and figuratively speaking.

5. WHY MONEY CREATION BY PRIVATE BANKS?

A legacy of history

Money creation by private banks is a legacy of history. Banking started around the 15th, 16th century when goldsmiths started storing gold for their clients. To prove ownership customers received certificates which came to be used as a means of payment. Initially the goldsmiths gave out as many certificates as they had gold in stock, but they soon realized it was very unlikely that all customers would demand their gold at the same time. So they issued more certificates than they had gold in their vaults: money creation through private banking was born. For banks today the same applies as for goldsmiths at the time: if all customers demand their deposits at the same time - a so-called "bank run" - the bank will not be able to pay and will fail. And worse, depositors will loose their money.

An effective lobby

Over the past two centuries, in countries where money creation took place by central banks and thus by government bankers have used all their influence to push for privatizing money creation. In some countries, especially the United States, that's been a tough but ultimately successful battle. To such an extent that the current US central bank, the Federal Reserve, is partly owned by private banks. In practice, therefore, the Fed functions as a kind of public-private partnership which represents the interests of the general public as well as the banks.

Whereas in the US the battle for control over the money supply was an arduous one, in some cases pitting presidents or presidential candidates against the most prominent bankers, in other countries the privatization of money creation has gone virtually unnoticed. Either way the outcome has been the same: today in all developed and almost all developing countries money is created by private banks. Perhaps the most remarkable feature of this situation is that the question of whether money creation should be a public or private function is asked no longer.

A matter of trust

As is the case with money the whole concept of banking is based on trust: the belief that the bank will be able to pay out whenever the client demands it. If that trust wanes and large numbers of depositors all demand their money at the same time the bank will fail. In the past, before the 1930s, this happened frequently, with serious consequences for the economy if major banks were involved. To avoid bank runs and thereby bank failures the US government created deposit guarantees, with which the state guarantees the deposits of private individuals and companies up to a specified amount. Deposit insurance has been an effective instrument in maintaining confidence in the ability of private banks to pay out the deposits of their customers, thus avoiding the bank runs that would lead to the guarantee having to be honoured.

6. DRAWBACKS OF OUR SYSTEM

Private money creation: from crisis to crisis

There are many reasons to change the current system. To begin with, the current system works less well than its advocates would have us believe. Exhibit number one: the financial crisis of 2008. That crisis is no exception: since the 1980s there have been dozens of large and small financial crises.[8] Apparently the market works less well than many economists and other market adepts would have us believe.

Economic theory: financial markets cannot work

It's remarkable that economic theory teaches implicitly that financial markets cannot function well. According to that theory the "invisible hand of the market", a concept conceived by the 18th century scholar Adam Smith, ensures that private undertakings benefit society as a whole when three conditions are met. First, economic actors, meaning people, must always make economically rational decisions. Second, people must be fully informed: they must have all knowledge relevant for making a decision making. And third, there must be perfect competition – meaning an infinite number of producers and consumers.

In the real world, and especially in financial markets, none of these conditions are met. People do not act in an economically rational manner: social, psychological, biological and cultural factors also influence behaviour. Also, the banking sector is not particularly competitive: in many countries there are only a limited number of players, big banks that hold a large part of the market. And it may be difficult to prove, but it often appears that there are tacit agreements to limit competition – for example, by not competing too

---

[8] The IMF counted, between 1970 and 2010, 425 banking, sovereign debt and monetary crises (cited among others in Lietaer, B.A., Arnsperger, C., Goerner, S. & Brunnhuber, S. (2012). Money and sustainability : the missing link ; a report from the Club of Rome – EU Chapter to Finance Watch and the World Business Academy. Axminster: Triarchy Press with The Club of Rome.

aggressively on the interest rate paid on savings or the interest charged on loans.

The most important inhibiting factor for markets "doing their work" is that many operators, from small consumers to governments, lack information. Most people not only have no idea of how our monetary system works but also lack understanding of all kinds of financial products. Many even have trouble understanding their own financial situation. For example, a study estimated four out of five people in the Netherlands were unable to judge the benefits and risks of financial products – and that was the best score among the 13 countries surveyed.[9]

In short, the basic conditions for the proper functioning of markets, established by economic science itself, are not met for financial markets (as well as many other ones). Yet the belief prevails that the market, in the form of a system of profit-oriented private banks, is the best way to control money creation and allocation.

Private banks: a brake on money creation?

Faith in markets for controlling our money supply is mainly based on the idea that the market itself sets limits on the amount of money being created. Governments, so it is argued, can add to the money supply without limit, but private banks cannot do so because they cannot provide indefinite amounts of credit: they can and will lend and thus create money only if they are fairly certain the loan is repaid.

Because there are limits to what banks can lend it is assumed they cannot cause an explosion in the money supply. That's true only in part. Since the 1990s banks have created huge amounts of virtual money that ended up largely in financial markets. These form a kind of virtual economy with few ties to the "real" economy of the production and consumption of goods and services. Much of the money thus created ended up in complex financial products – famously called "financial weapons of mass-destruction" by

---

[9] Study discussed in the Dutch newspaper De Volkskrant, December 23, 2009

American billionaire and "super-investor" Warren Buffett. These products were the basis for the 2008 financial crisis. Post- crisis, after a brief downturn, growth in this speculative financial system has resumed as before, leading to an ever growing risk of a new crisis.

Many economists believe that these problems can be controlled by regulation. Over the past centuries that assumption has been made time and again, after which yet again things went wrong and the next crisis was born. It therefore appears that even with regulation the system is inherently unstable.

Our current monetary system: no way out of the crisis

So where has our current monetary system brought us? The effects of the crisis are still with us. Governments and many citizens are deeply in debt, disposable income is declining, and unemployment is growing or at best, hardly decreasing. Entitlements are reduced, costs for basic services such as education and health care are on the rise. In many countries the national infrastructure is in poor shape, even crumbling, as there is little or no money for maintenance, let alone improvement. And there is barely money for investment for the future, such as reducing greenhouse gas emissions through energy efficiency and the switch to renewable energy.

Money to the financial economy

It's not as if there is an absolute shortage of money. The problem is that banks and other financial players pump most of the money into the financial or virtual economy, where it is used for speculation rather than production and consumption.[10] At the same time the "real" economy of the production and consumption of goods and services faces a money shortage.

---

[10] Monetary expert Bernard Lietaer estimated for 2010 that of the 4 trillion dollar traded daily in currency transactions only 2% was of significance for the "real" economy, e.g. for importing or exporting goods and services; the other 98% was used purely for speculation. See Bernard Lietaer et al., *Money and Sustainability. The Missing Link*, 2012; Report of the Club of Rome.

Even if central banks create money to remedy the shortage of money in the real economy, through so-called quantitative easing[11], the effects are limited if not counterproductive. That's because in the current monetary system central banks cannot channel money directly into the economy: that is left to private banks. In an economic downturn these banks see more opportunities for making money in financial markets, through speculation. Therefore banks allocate a much larger part of the newly created money to the financial economy than to the real one. This creates new bubbles in financial markets and in housing prices, thus laying the foundations for the next financial crisis. At the same time the money in the real economy remains scarce, resulting in much production capacity lying idle, with bankruptcies and unemployment as a result.

Banking: socialism for the rich

Another disadvantage is that if things go wrong the government must intervene: the banks must be saved. This applies especially to the so-called "too big to fail" banks, of which it is feared that should they fail they'd take down the entire financial system and thereby, the economy. To prevent this from happening the government spends huge sums of money on nationalizing or supporting banks that are about to fail. And since the government is funded through taxation it's the taxpayer who foots the bill.

At the same time the national debt increases due to the many billions of dollars spent on the bail-outs. The loans for doing so are partly provided by the same banks that caused the crisis, meaning new money is created that is lent to the government at an interest rate that gives the banks a tidy profit. The money for repaying the loan plus interest must, once more, be raised by taxpayers.

Indirectly, the taxpayer also pays a price: to reduce the deficits created by the bank bail-outs the government has to reduce

---

[11] Quantitative easing is a central bank policy aiming to stimulate the economy. It involves central banks buying financial assets from commercial banks and other private institutions, thus increasing the supply of money available for consumption and investment.

spending, as a result of which services are cut or become more expensive.

In summary: if all goes well with the banks the (ample) profits are for the shareholders, managers and financial traders, in the form of dividends, exorbitant salaries and bonuses. If things go wrong the losses are passed on to ordinary citizens. This has been described as privatizing profits and socializing losses, or socialism for the rich.

Private money creation: ups and downs

The current monetary system leads to an economic see-saw with high peaks and deep troughs in economic performance, or, as economists call it, the business cycle. The variations are aggravated by private banks because in good economic times they give more loans, as they see more opportunities for profit. This boosts the economy further, at some point leading to economic overheating, asset bubbles and a new crisis. Then, in times of economic contraction, banks are hesitant to lend money, meaning less money is created precisely at a time when more is needed for economic recovery. This behaviour of banks makes sense from a business point of view and is, therefore, in line with the logic of private banking. But it is contrary to the public interest, because the economy as a whole gets the opposite of what is needed.

A small group benefits from banking

Yet another drawback of the current system is that all the benefits of the privilege of creating money (with a technical term, *seigniorage*) end up with the aforementioned small group of people: bankers, traders, and bank shareholders. Why this is so has been explained already in the above: it has grown over the past few centuries – not least as a result of intensive lobbying by private bankers supported by the faith of standard economics in markets.

However, there is no reason to continue extending this privilege of money creation to a few privileged companies, executives and shareholders. We've already done so for the past two centuries, so why continue to provide a small elite with this boon? It would be much more logical and equitable to have the profits of that privilege benefit society as a whole, by bringing the right to create money back to where it belongs: the government.

Bank belly up, money gone

For savers a major drawback of the present system is that it exposes them to the risk of losing their money when the bank where they have their account fails. That's because the bank is allowed to put the deposits on the asset side of their balance sheet, meaning that from there on the money is counted as property of the bank, even though the obligation remains to return the money to the depositor when he or she claims it.[12] However, in a bankruptcy the bank will no longer be able to pay and depositors will loose their money, except for the part that is guaranteed by the state.

Credit, interest rate and debt

Perhaps the biggest problem of money creation by private banks is that it's inextricably linked to profit-oriented lending and thus, to debt and interest. Lending takes place only if the bank is convinced that in the future the borrower will be able to repay the borrowed capital plus interest. Therefore borrowing is possible only with an increase in profits (for companies), income (for consumers), and tax revenues (for government).

---

[12] It is an open question whether what banks are doing is legal: the British expert Richard Werner points out that in England, according to the "Client Money Rules", companies should always keep customer funds separate from equity, meaning they are not allowed to put it on their balance sheets. This may apply to other countries too. However, banks *are* permitted to put deposits on their balance sheets, exposing depositors to the risk of loosing their deposit if the bank goes under. Werner points out that the removal of this privilege of the banks by also forcing banks to adhere to the "Client Money Rules" would deprive banks of the privilege of money creation. Werner and other experts also point out that banks have no official mandate to create money: neither in the current manner nor in a different way. See Werner, RA, *How do banks create money, and why can other firms not do the same? An explanation for the coexistence of lending and deposit-taking.* Pre-publication; Publication expected in the International Review of Financial Analysis in 2015.

Debt leads to a growth imperative

More profit, earnings and tax revenues are inextricably linked to economic growth. Without growth there is no increase in company profits, consumer incomes and government revenues, and loans plus accumulated interest cannot be repaid. There is no or very little growth during an economic downturn, leading to many people, companies, and even countries no longer being able to meet their payment obligations. That can lead to a debt crisis, which is sometimes delayed by further borrowing. But this only increases the debts and thereby the problem. In consequence, without strong growth a new and possibly even graver crisis becomes almost inevitable. Many experts believe that, in the aftermath of the 2008 crisis, with many households, companies and countries (still) deep in debt, another major crisis is looming.

The growth imperative and finite resources

Lending, then, is tied to growth: growth is indispensable to repay debts plus interest. Besides growing indebtedness this causes another major problem: continuing growth can not be reconciled with the finite nature of our natural resources. The money supply can, in principle, grow indefinitely but our stocks of raw materials, fresh water, land, and natural ecosystems are finite. Economic growth is putting ever greater demands on those resources, in an unsustainable manner. Meaning that, if we continue present ways, we ourselves or future generations will face major shortfalls and run out of essential resources such as fresh water, agricultural land, metals, and fuel. This will cause huge problems especially for the have-nots in our world. The rich will be able to handle the price increases resulting from the shortages initially, but they too will ultimately suffer, especially if the deficits lead to popular uprisings.

Our monetary system and finite resources

The growth imperative and thereby, the unsustainable use of finite resources is inextricably linked to private money creation. In other words, the current monetary system will, sooner or later, cause shortages of finite resources. That in itself is enough reason to convert to another monetary system.

Besides the growth imperative there is another reason why the current monetary system is incompatible with the sustainable use of resources. The main objective and in many cases, the sole purpose of private banks is to maximize profits and not, as should be the case from a public interest point of view, to provide society with the money supply needed for an optimally functioning economy. Functioning optimally does not mean maximum wealth creation through maximum efficiency – the implicit and sometimes explicit purpose of mainstream economics. From a public interest perspective functioning optimally means achieving public goals as effectively and efficiently as possible. Goals such as providing in everyone's basic needs, creating equal opportunities for all, optimizing wellbeing, and the sustainable use of natural resources so they'll be available for both current and future generations. These goals are incompatible with the profit maximization of private banks.

Money creation only for profitable activities

The current monetary system, with money being created by commercial banks to make a profit, has resulted in the odd situation that money is created only for profitable activities. From a public interest perspective it may be very important for government to invest in, for example, better education, a healthier environment, good quality health care and disease prevention, and the development and application of renewable energy. But if such investments are not profitable no money is created for it. Instead the state has to raise money by taxing or borrowing. It can do so only to a limited extent because it has to finance so much more and, especially after the crisis, already lacks the money to do that.

Government as a parasitic entity

The peculiar situation of having given the privilege to create money to private banks thus leads to the situation that government, because of the fact it has to tax to raise money, is seen as a kind of parasitic entity living on the pockets of hard-working citizens and enterprises.

And in a sense with the current monetary system that is indeed the case. But this situation stems from our conscious or unconscious choice for our current monetary system in which the privilege of money creation is yielded to private banks. And it is the result of economic faith: the economic dogma of mainstream economics that has made a taboo of public money creation for direct use by government.

Fostering poverty and impoverishment

A final drawback of private money creation is that it contributes, indirectly, to poverty, deprivation and inequality. Lending money to poor people is not profitable, therefore little or no money is created for them. Even if it is interest rates are high because of the perceived risk of default and high administrative costs (ten small loans are more expensive to manage than one large loan). At the same time, as a result of the delegation of money creation to the private sector governments are withheld the money with which poverty and impoverishment could be addressed. This, of course, is not only a problem of our monetary system: addressing poverty also depends on political will. Yet the current monetary system complicates the political choice for poverty reduction because the needed funding cannot be created but must be raised by taxpayers.

Advantages of private money creation?

Are there any advantages to the current system? The first argument that its defenders will raise was already discussed: the assumption that with money creation by private banks the market mechanism will ensure the right amount of money is created. We've already seen that this is little more than a belief. It is true that the fact that banks only lend if they think the loan can be repaid with interest forms a brake on money creation. However, it's a brake does that not work well and is limited mainly to the real economy. Things are different in the financial or virtual economy. In financial markets there are almost unlimited possibilities of creating money for all sorts of speculation in financial products. Proof of this are the enormous quantities of money currently circulating in the financial markets.

Defenders of the current system will also argue that private banking has contributed to huge prosperity growth. This also is doubtful. First, as we shall see in the next chapter, both prosperity growth and well-being could have been much greater with the alternative to money creation by private banks, that is to say, with public money creation. Second, much of the wealth created through private banking is unsustainable because it derives from speculation. Such prosperity can indeed grow rapidly – until the next crisis occurs.

Proponents of private money creation and private enterprise in general will emphasize that only competition between multiple providers creates wealth-creating innovation. However, it was such innovative financial products that caused the crisis, showing that the results of this kind of innovation, even if highly profitable to those creating and selling the products, are rarely in line with the public interest. It is also a misconception that innovation is limited to the private sector. If that would be so then why do so many companies cooperate with public universities and research institutes, and contract them to do their research?

The defence of the present system

Our present monetary system, then, has many disadvantages and no clear advantages – except of course for bankers, traders, consultants, lobbyists, and private bank shareholders. Yet the system is firmly ingrained primarily because, as already indicated, the general public, the media, politicians, administrators and economists accept the current situation as an immutable given. The blame can be put with mainstream economics which, as a science, may be expected to engage in unbiased analysis and debate. However, very few economists seem to be interested in putting our monetary system up for discussion and thus support the status quo.

If the topic is brought up at all it is not so much to analyze in an objective manner the advantages and disadvantages of different monetary systems in support of political decision making. Instead it is attempted to stifle debate in the bud with the selective use of examples and unsound arguments. Alternative systems, in particular money creation by and for the government, are rejected out of hand with the argument that money creation by government will lead to financial and economic disaster. The favourite bogeyman is hyperinflation; the best known example is the hyperinflation in Germany in the 1920s. Ironically, sound historical research has led to the conclusion that although the German government did not go scot-free the hyperinflation was caused mainly by private banks. Also, usually not mentioned are the many examples of successful public money creation that did not lead to hyperinflation.

In the aforementioned IMF study of the Chicago Plan Benes and Kumhof demonstrate with many examples that generally, throughout history, governments have handled the privilege of money creation more responsibly than private banks. Major economic and financial problems, in the form of periods of excessive growth followed by a crisis and an economic downturn occurred primarily when the right to create money was granted to private parties.

Our Money – Towards a New Monetary System

7. HOW CAN WE DO BETTER?

The alternative: public money creation

A well-functioning monetary system is essential for a well-functioning economy and thereby, for the common good. The state is the agency responsible for the public interest. The responsibility for and control over the monetary system and money creation should therefore be placed with the state and not with private, profit-oriented enterprises. The logical alternative to money creation by private banks, therefore, is money creation by the state. In such a system it's not only coins and paper money that are created by the state but also the non-cash money now created by private banks. Meaning electronic money is then created by the same agency now responsible for coins and paper money.

Reform of the monetary system should lead to a more transparent management of the money supply with as its primary aim the short and long term common good, not private profit. Under the new system the responsibility for money creation would rest with a public monetary authority acting according to statutory objectives and guidelines. Such an authority already exists in most countries: the central bank. It would therefore be logical to give the money creation mandate to the central bank. In the following the terms monetary authority and central bank are used interchangeably.

At the same time the right of private banks to create money would be taken away. Banks would no longer, as presently, be able to create money by the simple accounting exercise linked to lending. Rather than creating their own money they would have to work with money created by the central bank. Such money would come from deposits, money borrowed from the central bank or in financial markets, and the bank's equity. Banking would be limited to the role that most people think banks perform today: managing the money of depositors by lending it to people and businesses willing to borrow it.

Money created by the monetary authority would be channelled into the economy in several ways. Directly by transferring the money to government to finance part of public spending, in particular investments. And indirectly by making the money available to banks for lending on to consumers and businesses.

Public or private banking?

Whether in addition to money creation by the central bank the task of bringing it into the economy should also become a public service is a separate topic of discussion. Many monetary reformers emphasize that monetary reform involves only the separation of the functions of money creation and money distribution. Existing private banks would continue banking, though no longer with money they would create themselves. However, there are good arguments for combining monetary reform with a public banking system. Public banks would ensure lending would be aimed less at maximizing profits for shareholders and more at public goals such as support to small and medium enterprises, job creation, and environmentally beneficial investments. Commercial, profit-oriented banking would not necessarily be banned: one can imagine a mixed system of public, private non-profit and private commercial banks in order to foster competition and thereby, service provision. It would be important to limit the size of both public and private banks to make sure there would be enough suppliers to guarantee genuine competition.

Advantages of public money creation

There are many advantages to a monetary system based on public money creation: a central bank / monetary authority making newly created, debt free money available to the state. It would resolve the debt problems of governments and thereby the current crisis as the government would no longer need to borrow money. The current public debt could be paid off gradually without having to cut back on public expenditure. This would make more money available for government investment in sectors such as education, health care, research, infrastructure, environment, and safety, creating jobs and growth.

Public money creation would also allow directing private investment. An example would be promoting private investments contributing to a sustainable use of resources, in the form of grants or interest free loans for companies that develop green technology.

Whether the benefit of money creation would be invested for the public good would be a political choice. Cabinet and parliament could also opt to channel those benefits to citizens and businesses by lowering taxes, increasing benefits and reducing public service fees.

Some monetary reformers propose, after the transition to public money creation, giving every citizen a one-time payment, a "citizen's dividend". This would become possible since as a result of the transition all "debt money" previously created by private banks would become state money. Citizens would be required to use this money to pay off their debts. Everyone would get an equal amount; the total amount paid would be equal to the total debt of all citizens. Because some citizens have more debts than others some would still be in debt, though much less so than before, whereas others would have money to spare.

Some reformers propose a dividend only for citizens, others, such as the proponents of the Chicago Plan, suggest a dividend for all debts other than those spent on capital goods (such as buildings and machinery). Including companies would be especially beneficial for small and medium enterprises, for some of which relief from a sizeable part or all debt could mean the difference between survival and bankruptcy.

Payment of a citizen's dividend could carry the risk of large numbers of people and businesses having money left wanting to spend it fast. This could lead to such a large increase in the demand for goods and services that producers would see an opportunity to raise their prices. If this would happen on a large scale, across economic sectors, this would result in an overall rise in prices: inflation. To prevent this some proponents of the Chicago Plan propose not to pay out any money remaining after all debt has been cancelled, but to deposit that remainder into a kind of investment fund. The returns generated by the fund would be paid out to the owner. This would mean much smaller payments spread over a prolonged period.

In practice the benefits of public money creation would probably be used to finance a mixture of policies: paying of government debt, public investment, tax cuts and a citizen's dividend. The focus would depend on the political orientation of the government: conservatives would be more inclined to have citizens and businesses benefit whereas social democrats would be likely to put more emphasis on public investment to address environmental and social concerns.

An end to the growth imperative

Public money creation would remove the drive for economic growth that is inextricably linked to private money creation. That would open the way to the transition to a stable economy in which the future can be secured through the sustainable use of finite resources.

A more stable economy

Another advantage of public money creation is that it would help to reduce the ups and downs in the economy that have marked the past centuries. As previously indicated these highs and lows are exacerbated by private banks which in good times boost the economy by too much lending and speculation, usually ending in a crisis. Conversely, in times of economic contraction they lend and thus create too little money, exactly when more money is needed for economic recovery. Public money creation, particularly when combined with public banking, would put an end to this phenomenon and would generally ensure that sufficient money enters the economy to make it function properly.

Less speculation, no more bail-outs

Public money creation would curtail the speculation that, even after the 2008 crisis, has been creating new financial bubbles, thereby laying the basis for the next crisis.[13] Banks getting into trouble

---

[13] The huge amounts of money circulating in the financial markets would not disappear right off in the transition to a new system, so large scale speculation would continue for the time being. But the amounts of money involved would grow much more slowly, stagnate or diminish because private banks could no longer create money for speculation. In the meantime central banks and governments would jointly look at ways to

through such speculation would no longer need to be rescued by the state and thus, the taxpayer. A bankruptcy of a big financial player would only have unpleasant consequences for those directly involved but not, as now, threaten the entire financial system and global economy.

Fewer risks, savings safe

Overall the risk of bank failures would be reduced because banks would manage only their own money and the deposits entrusted to them: it would no longer be possible to create large amounts of money by lending for speculation, with all the risks involved in the latter. Thus banks would become more stable and secure.

At the same time a significant advantage for savers would be that their deposits would be safe. As indicated earlier a saver now looses his money in case of a bankruptcy of the bank where he parked his money, except for the part guaranteed by government. Under the new system deposits would get the same status as shares or other securities managed by banks today. These remain the property of the owner even if the bank fails. In the new system this would also be the case for savings, meaning government guarantees would no longer be necessary.

Transparency

Finally, the new system would ensure that money creation and allocation are much more transparent and therefore more controllable. The current disproportionate influence of the financial sector on society and politics would decrease, with less pressure on

---

gradually reduce the enormous amounts of money circulating in the financial markets. How to achieve this would probably vary by type of financial product. Measures should be taken to avoid large amounts of speculation money flowing to the real economy as that could raise demand to such an extent that it could lead to inflation. This problem might be smaller than assumed as the massive selling off of financial products would cause their price to plummet. Speculation in financial markets could be reduced further with a tax on financial transactions, the so-called Tobin tax, named after a well-known American economist and Nobel laureate.

decision makers to represent the interests of the financial sector at the expense of the public interest.

Risks of public money creation

What are the risks of money creation by the state? Defenders of the current system often indicate that governments are prone to abuse the privilege and would create too much money, causing inflation. This would be a genuine risk if those deciding on money creation would be exposed to political influence. Politicians, to humour voters and satisfy special interest groups could exert pressure to create more money than warranted. The solution to this problem was already given: eliminate political influence by giving the monetary authority the status of an independent entity that cannot be subjected to political pressure.[14] Thus decision making on the money supply would be based only on technical criteria and remain in line with the authority's mandate.

Central bank independence already exists in almost all developed countries. To the extent necessary this autonomy could be confirmed through legislation. The central bank could thus acquire the status of what some experts have called a "fourth power": an institution with its own mandate, autonomy and responsibility, as the other three branches of power: executive, legislative and judicial.

The risk remains that too much money would be created if those responsible at the central bank / monetary authority would overestimate the economy's productive capacity. This could lead to a situation in which producers would feel that they could raise prices at will because their products would be sold anyway. Such price increases could raise the overall price level causing unwanted inflation: so-called "demand-pull inflation", or demand inflation for short.

On the other hand employees might raise their wage demands if they became aware of higher prices as well as the fact that employers

---

[14] The British organization for monetary reform, Positive Money, suggests a "Monetary Creation Committee", comparable to the present Monetary Policy Committee of the British central bank, the Bank of England.

would be competing for their labour. Employers might yield to such demands if they perceived they could pass on the extra cost to the buyers of their product by raising prices. Suppliers of raw materials and semi-finished products or components could also increase their prices in the expectation that their buyers – the makers of the end products – would pay them anyway. The resulting overall increase in price levels is called "cost-push inflation", cost inflation for short.

Demand-pull and cost-push inflation could result in a so-called "wage-price spiral", in which the two types of inflation coincide in pushing up prices. This phenomenon occurred in the 1970s and came to an end only after a severe economic downturn in the early 1980s. It is, therefore, something to be avoided.

Preventing demand and cost inflation

In general the monetary authority would prevent demand and cost inflation by making sure the amount of money added to the existing money supply would not be such that the demand it would generate would exceed the productive capacity of the economy. This could be achieved among others by government projects and programs not being awarded to private companies charging higher prices than warranted. In cases in which all parties making a bid would overcharge the activities to be funded should be postponed until they could be contracted at a reasonable price.[15] Such policies would also restrain excessive wage demands in the productive sectors concerned.

Overall excessive wage demands in both private and public sector should be avoided too. To start with, before the transition to public money creation employers, employees and other stakeholders should be briefed thoroughly on both the benefits of public money creation

---

[15] Such a course of action would require a different way of government budgeting. Now there is often the urge to spend a budget because if not the money involved will be reclaimed by the treasury. This may lead to a lower budget allocation in the following year. Thus in the current situation careful management by postponing expenditures is punished - something that needs to change even if government would not be able to create its own money.

and its preconditions – notably, restraint on the part of workers and producers in wage and price demands. Agreements on the latter should be developed with, and signed by all parties. Thereafter there should be regular rounds of consultation to adapt those agreements to changing circumstances.

It may be expected that with a public monetary system and responsible behaviour on the part of producers and workers inflation would decrease and possibly disappear. That's because as stated earlier central banks currently aim at inflation of around two percent to promote economic growth; growth that is necessary to meet debt obligations. In a system of public money creation system debt would be greatly reduced, meaning that growth and inflation would no longer be needed. The aim would be to attain price stability and thereby, savings maintaining their value.

Transition

What would the transition from private to public money creation look like? Andrew Jackson and Ben Dyson of the English organization Positive Money, the leading British organization in the field of monetary reform, chart the transition in a book titled *Modernising Money*. [16]. They describe two phases. The first phase involves the overnight transition to the new system when the new regulations for money creation and credit become law and the necessary accounting adjustments are made on the balance sheets of banks and government.

In the second phase, which could last from ten to twenty years, the debt created under the old system is repaid gradually, with existing money or money created by the central bank under the new system. The Positive Money publication describes this process as recovering from the "debt hangover". Government debt could be repaid according to schedule with newly created central bank money.

---

[16] The following link provides an overview of the contents of the book: http://www.positivemoney.org/wp-content/uploads/2013/01/Modernising-Money-Free-Overview.pdf

Private debts could be paid from the aforementioned "citizen's dividend" and money from the regular money supply.

Mandate of the monetary authority

After the transition the monetary authority decides on the amount of new money to be created. The mandate of this authority, as that of the central bank, is to be established by law, and will amount to the double function of preventing inflation and ensuring an optimal money supply. This translates into a money supply that is adequate for meeting both public needs and the demand for money from individual citizens and businesses, in a manner that prevents inflation and makes optimal use of the productive capacity of the economy. This implies that the money supply and thereby overall demand is limited to a level where producers meet total demand without raising their prices.

Channelling new money into the economy

As indicated newly created money would be brought into the economy through government and banks. The government could do so in several ways: through government spending, direct payments to citizens, such as the aforementioned citizen's dividend, and by paying off government debt. Another possibility is tax cuts, with newly created money compensating for lower tax revenues.

Government and parliament would decide which of these forms would be used and to what extent. The monetary authority and government would cooperate closely to align and coordinate money creation, the generation of government income in other ways such as taxation, and public expenditure.

8. OBSTACLES AND SOLUTIONS

Inflation phobia

The main obstacle for public money creation has already been mentioned in the above: the fear that the creation of money by government will lead, sooner or later, to large scale inflation. Governments, it is thought, will be unable to restrain themselves, resulting in the excess creation of money, too much money entering the economy, and inflation. We've already discussed how this danger can be countered: by delegating money creation to an independent monetary authority.

A bigger problem is the belief of mainstream economists and in their wake, politicians, the media and other pundits in the quantity theory of money. As said this theory parts from the premise that the existing money supply is already in balance with supply and demand. It is therefore thought that even a small increase in the money supply that's not market driven would lead to inflation. As with much other economic theory there is no factual proof that this theory holds, on the contrary. Yet it has become economic dogma, with among its most dedicated followers the German monetary authorities. Germans in general suffer from a strong case of inflation phobia as a result of the already mentioned hyperinflation in the country in the 1920s. Hence the only goal of the German central bank and, under German influence, the European central bank is controlling inflation. By comparison the US central bank, the Federal Reserve, has a dual objective: fighting inflation and fighting unemployment.

Is it true that the risk of (hyper) inflation is higher with public than with private money creation? Historical research has shown systems based on private money creation lead to more and more severe financial and economic crises, including bouts of hyperinflation. Linking the fear of high inflation to public money creation is therefore unjustified. Which, of course, does not remove the need to structure a new monetary system in such a way that inflation is kept under control. In a system where a public monetary authority is responsible for money creation the opportunities to do so are much greater than in the current, privately managed system.

Private money creation as economic dogma

In current economic thinking money creation by and for the state is a taboo. Mainstream economists assume that only market forces can ensure that the right amount of money is created. Especially right-wing economists place their faith in market self-regulation and preach *laissez faire*: let the market do its work without being hindered by regulation. The middle and the left are more inclined to various forms of regulation. But the belief that the economy as a whole and money creation in particular should be left to the private sector and thereby the market is untouchable. It is one of the primary tenets of the economic church. In consequence alternatives such as public money creation are not even considered in mainstream economics, not even after a financial and economic crisis that was due largely to irresponsible lending and thus, private money creation.

The real cause of inflation

As indicated creating too much money indeed can cause inflation because as a result of excessive demand producers and workers exact higher prices and wages. And there is an even greater risk: loss of confidence, that is, the loss of the belief that money will retain its value.

The cause of hyperinflation is not so much the creation of excessive amounts of money as a loss of confidence. The German hyperinflation is a good example. Accounts from that period invariably mention that the printing presses could not keep up with inflation, meaning they could not print the money fast enough, which signifies the money lost its value *before* it was made. The printing of money, therefore, was not a cause but a consequence of hyperinflation.

You don't have to look far to realize that the quantity of money in itself is of little significance. Both before and after the 2008 financial crisis excessive credit, speculation and all kinds of exotic financial products led to the creation of huge amounts of money – much more than was justified by the increase in output and demand in the "real" economy. It's safe to say, therefore, that both pre- and post crisis too much money was put into circulation. Yet inflation remains low. There is even fear of deflation: an increase in the value of money because the overall price level drops.

This shows it's perfectly possible to have a major increase in the money supply without causing inflation – as long as this larger money supply does not translate into an excessive demand for goods and services in the real economy. If that happens producers and workers are likely to increase prices and wage demands, leading to demand-pull and cost-push inflation. This did not happen in recent decades because the excessive amounts of money created did not end up in the real but in the financial economy, where it was used for the kinds of speculation that caused the crisis.

Maintaining confidence

To prevent (hyper) inflation with public money creation, then, requires two things. On the one hand adding to the money supply should not create more demand than the productive sectors of the economy can handle. Second, the general public must be confident that money will keep its value. For both conditions the best guarantee is delegating decision making about money creation to an independent, technically competent monetary authority that inspires confidence – such as the central bank.

However, the value of money is determined not only by users but also, and perhaps more so, on the international financial markets. To maintain confidence in a currency based on public money creation may prove to be the greater challenge.

Can the transition be made in one country?

Many advocates of monetary reform, including the experts of Positive Money, think it's possible to have the transition to public money creation take place in a single country. They arrive at this conclusion on the basis of a rational analysis of the economic impact of the transition. However, it remains to be seen how financial markets would react to the announcement of a country planning the transition, or even to the rumour that a country would consider it.

IMF experts Benes and Kumhof also argue that the economic benefits of a new monetary system, in their case the Chicago Plan, are such that the financial markets would not constitute a danger to the country making the transition. They do discuss the possibility of an "irrational speculative attack" after the transition and advice on measures to be taken against such an attack. However, they do not discuss the above mentioned greater danger of such an attack before transition, based only on the transition having been announced or rumoured. That is the greater danger, because such a response would likely be more of a psychological than of a rational economic nature. The greatest danger would be herd behaviour by traders. Some holders of the currency of the country making the transition would, in line with economic dogma, fear that the currency involved would decline rapidly in value and therefore want to get rid of it as soon as possible. Other traders would get wind of this and also become afraid of a drop in value, leading them also to sell the currency involved. In consequence the value would indeed fall, and more quickly as more traders would behave similarly. A self-fulfilling prophecy would result: because traders would expect a decrease in the value of the currency they would engage in the behaviour that would actually cause such a decrease.

To avoid the risk of such a panic in the financial markets it would appear sensible to make the transition in several countries at once, preferably by a majority of countries with internationally accepted, "strong" currencies. This would also allow central banks to coordinate with other central banks the decision making on the amounts of money to be created in different currencies. These days national economies and financial systems have become so intertwined that in any case, decision making on money creation would best be done collectively.

A transition in several countries at once would require an international conference on the establishment of a new financial system. This has been done before: in the last year of World War II, when representatives from 44 countries met in Bretton Woods in the

US to agree on the rules, institutions and procedures to regulate post-war international finance. Something similar should be done now.

Psychological obstacles

Besides inflation phobia there are other obstacles that block the creation of a new financial system. These are of a more psychological nature. People, and therefore societies are risk-averse and therefore conservative: we are hesitant to replace something existing with something new. That certainly applies to something as important as our monetary system. That caution is even greater if things are going relatively well - and in developed countries that is, despite the crisis, for most people still the case.

The willingness to change is even smaller if we are not aware of there being a good alternative. And even then there will be suspicion towards something that seems as simple and "too good to be true" as public money creation. As said, the idea that money can just be "made" out of thin air and provided to the state or to companies and citizens is alien to us. It's against our culture: money must be earned before it can be spent.

Overcoming psychological barriers

In order to overcome these psychological obstacles it's important to think once again about the character of money. We must keep in mind that money is merely a symbol which serves as the (electronic) lubricant of our economy. We can make as much of it as we need, within the aforementioned limits of maintaining confidence and demand remaining in line with production capacity. We should remember in particular that there is no reason to refrain from addressing society's environmental, social and economic challenges society because ostensibly there is no money to do so. There is no absolute lack of money, or if there is it can be resolved in no time. What "there is no money" implies is that the state, the institution looking after our common good, does not have the money. That, in turn, is the outcome of our choice for a monetary system in which the privilege and benefits of money creation are yielded to private banks.

Another important way to overcome our psychological barriers to change is to look around us. We then see that left and right companies go bankrupt and public services are downsized or eliminated. This includes companies and services that could provide the goods and services with which to tackle our environmental and social problems effectively. At the same time people lose their jobs, unemployment and economic uncertainty are growing, and large numbers of young people are unable to find steady, reasonably paying employment. When observing this we need to realize again that this is due to the fact that we have opted for delegating the control over the money supply and the right to create money to profit-oriented enterprises. In other words, to our choice for a monetary system that not only brought us the 2008 crisis and many before it all over the world, but also blocks us from addressing our social problems and by doing so, working our way out of the crisis.

We can argue that we have not made the choice for our current monetary system consciously. But we can no longer use this as an excuse when we are aware of both that choice and of the alternative.

Influence of the banks: money is power

Besides inflation phobia and conservatism there is another factor that hinders the transition to public money creation: the vested interests of the financial sector, banks in particular. Especially the huge "too-big-to-fail banks" have enormous political influence and use it to promote bank-friendly legislation. Moreover, in a country such as the United States there is a revolving door between

---

[17] For 2014 the Center for Responsive Politics reports for Washington for the financial industry (securities, investment and insurance) a total of some 1600 confirmed lobbyists; expenditure by the sector amounted to about $ 250,000,000.
(https://www.opensecrets.org/lobby/top.php?indexType=i&showYear=2014). Corporate Europe Observatory indicates in a 2014 report that at European Community HQ in Brussels the financial sector employs some 1700 lobbyists to influence decision making on financial issues, with a total budget of € 123,000,000.
(http://corporateeurope.org/sites/default/files/attachments/financial_lobby_report.pdf)

government and large banks: elected officials and public servants in key positions often come from large internationally operating banks, particularly the infamous investment bank Goldman Sachs. After a stint as a public servant the individuals involved usually return to the financial sector. Thus private banking interests are strongly represented at the heart of government.

And that's not mentioning the billions spent by banks on lobbyists, who are expected to push decision makers and members of parliament into approving legislation favourable to banks and blocking or mitigating legislation that is seen as harmful to financial interests.[17]

The enormous influence of the financial lobby is shown by the fact that the largest US banks, largely responsible for the financial crisis of 2008, have had to pay only minor damages in comparison to the damage caused. Even in cases where banks were fined and damages paid the amounts involved were only a fraction of what the banks earned with the practices for which they were fined. In almost all cases those amounts were part of an arrangement that freed the banks from having to plead guilty. Not one of those responsible has gone to jail.

At least the US has done something: other countries have done nothing at all, or worse, are blocking measures to reign in the sector. The prime example is the UK, where the financial sector ("The City") is of such importance to the economy that the British government is doing everything it can to block European measures to get a somewhat greater hold on the banks. Money is power, and the ability to create money only increases the power of the financial sector.

Economic dogma protects financial system and banks

It may be expected, then, that the financial sector will do its utmost to block the transition to a new system in which they would loose the financial benefits linked to money creation. Yet banks are fortunate in that it's hardly necessary for them to engage in the fight against public money creation. For that they can count on economic science: the belief of economists and in their wake, policy makers, politicians and the media that only markets can determine the right amount of money for the economy. It is the belief that no man, group or organization can match Adam Smith's invisible hand of the market. This dogma of market infallibility is an even bigger obstacle to change than the power of the financial sector. For mainstream economics not only idealizes the market but also, and in line with the faith, is sceptical about government. On the one hand because the state is not subject to market discipline and therefore to the restraint exercised by the invisible hand. On the other because actions of government usually involve some kind of market interference, which is perceived as a threat to the perfect balance of the market that especially conservative economists so ardently believe in. Thus the practitioners of conventional economics, consciously or unconsciously, form the first, formidable defence against change.

Breaking the power of the financial sector

But if fractures occur in that line of defence, if at least part of the economics profession is able to look beyond the dogmas of their science and start thinking seriously about another financial system "for the people, by the people", it can be expected that the financial sector will throw everything it has into the fight to maintain the current system. It will, therefore, be a tough fight, but it should be possible to overcome the influence and power of the financial sector. After all, only a small group of people benefits from the current system and would loose from the transition to a new financial system based on public money creation. It's only those traders and bank managers who in addition to already high salaries receive or award huge bonuses to themselves and their colleagues, and speculators who are lucky enough to make money from the ups and downs in the financial markets. This group amounts to at most a few tens of thousands of people.

Shareholders of banks also would be likely to suffer from the transition to a new monetary system, as bank profitability would be reduced to the level of normal enterprises. In consequence bank stock would almost certainly loose value if the financial boon resulting from the ability to create money out of thin air is taken away. Among those shareholders will be institutions that serve a public purpose, notably pension funds. However, under a new monetary system these organizations could be compensated for this decline in the value of their bank stock.[18]

---

[18] A major question is whether under a new monetary system pension funds should continue to exist in their current form. With public money creation the need for mandatory pension saving would disappear or diminish. The problem would no longer be, as now, that without a pensions saving system pensions have to be paid from current worker contributions and taxes ("pay as you go"), leading to an increasing drain on worker's payrolls and government budgets especially in countries with graying populations. With public money creation government would have more financial leeway to pay pensions because much public investment would no longer be financed through taxes but through money creation. The challenge would no longer be a monetary one but rather, to ensure that sufficient goods and services are produced to meet the needs and demands of both workers and non-workers. That challenge already exists in countries with graying populations but is obscured by the ongoing debate on the financial aspect: the size of pensions and other benefits, their coverage and whether or not to compensate for inflation. Public money creation would allow a shift of focus because the financial dimension would become much less important. Thus policy makers, science and industry could focus on the real task, which is or should not be money but the challenge of meeting, with a diminishing work force, the growing demand for goods and services from the non-working population the working population and government. That's not a question of money but of production capacity, of the more effective and efficient use of the available labor and technology.

Abolishing or greatly diminishing the size of pension funds would have another advantage: it would sharply reduce the amount of money that flows into financial markets in search of yields. The large scale (obligatory) saving for pensions contributes hugely to too much money chasing too few investment opportunities: the recipe for a financial crisis. This problem already plays today but would be even greater if all countries would establish "responsible" pension systems such as those of Denmark, Sweden, Australia, Switzerland, The Netherlands and Canada, and to a somewhat lesser extent the UK and US. Most European countries, including France, Italy, and even solid Germany have partial pay-as-you-go-systems in which a large proportion of pensions is paid directly from the state budget. In the coming years, due to aging populations and the current monetary system,

Everyone else would benefit from public money creation. Citizens would enjoy more, better and cheaper public services, tax cuts, lower debt and possibly, a citizens' dividend. Governments would be able to invest much more for the future and thus, for future generations. Producers, especially of goods and services required for the transition to a more sustainable society and economy, would benefit from increased government demand. Small and medium enterprises would benefit from the increased demand from government and consumers. Public money creation would also greatly improve access to credit, especially if combined with a public banking system. And due to increased demand and economic activity many of the currently unemployed would be able to go back to work, if need be after retraining.

One would expect that with so many benefits for such a large proportion of the population it should be possible to generate a massive popular movement and overcome the vested interests of a small group, however powerful and influential.

Our biggest mistake: delegation

Perhaps the biggest obstacle to change is that we leave something as crucial as thinking about and deciding on our monetary system to those we consider knowledgeable. We figure we know too little, it's their job, and accept what they say. If they do not question the current system, who are we to do so?

---

this will lead to major financial challenges for the countries involved. On the other hand, if France, Italy and Germany and a range of other countries with pay-as-you-go systems would have pension systems as the earlier mentioned nations, the amount of money in search of yields in financial markets would increase hugely without a rise in investment opportunities. Put simply, (pension) fund managers would not know what to do with all that money. The conclusion is that current pension systems are incompatible with the actual monetary system. On the one hand because broad international application of pension savings schemes would lead to excessive hoarding of money. On the other, because a pay-as-you-go pension system is unaffordable in a monetary system in which money creation is tied to debt and interest.

The problem is that, as we have already seen, the experts do not come up with better alternatives for our money system. Not because economists consciously keep us from addressing the problems society faces: most believe sincerely that the current system of private money creation is best for us. They feel this way because their education and professional careers have given them a distorted picture of reality and tunnel vision. In consequence few economists are aware of the limitations and misconceptions of their science and of the policy recommendations based on them, and fewer still are able to see economic reality from a different perspective than that ingrained by their faith.

That is not to say that there are no critical economists who question certain components and assumptions of their science. However, this is a minority that thus far has had little impact on professional practice and even less on policy making. And even most members of this group do not go so far as to question the dogmas of their faith. Yet it's precisely there where the problem lies.[19]

---

[19] Further substantiation of this critique of mainstream economics and its practitioners will be given in the booklet *Economy: science or faith?* (in preparation). A detailed explanation is found in the book *Crisis, Economics, and the Emperor's Clothes* (Frans Doorman, 2012), which indicates why mainstream economics fails as science, the consequences of that failure, and what should be done about it. The book can be ordered in hardcopy on www.lulu.com, and can be downloaded for free as a pdf from www.new-economics.info.

Our Money – Towards a New Monetary System

9. WHAT TO DO?

Opening the debate

We need a serious public and political debate on the pros and cons of the current monetary system, the alternative of public money creation described in this booklet, and on how system change might happen. In particular, because many experts tell us the next crisis is already in the making. The consequences of such a crisis will be even more severe than those of the 2008 crisis. On the one hand because the latter is far from over, on the other because under the present monetary system governments will no longer have the means to limit the fall-out of such a collapse. Political parties but also civil society – trade unions, environmental organizations, associations representing the interests of small and medium enterprises – should insist on such a debate. The media should play an important role in facilitating such a discussion. Economists who are willing to think and work on developing alternatives can play a key role. Economists unable to push themselves beyond the out-of-hand rejection of system change and blocking an open discussion should, after being heard, be ignored.

Discussion based on arguments

We, ordinary citizens, should not allow ourselves to be excluded from the debate by people pretending to have all the answers, even if they are high-ranking academics, officials or otherwise enjoy high status and prestige. We will have to part from the premise that economists, although very intelligent and clever, are so deformed by their training and profession that rather than practicing science they proclaim a faith: the belief that the market will put things right. We cannot hinge decision making on our monetary system, our economy, our society and our future on the tenets and dogmas of a science with such serious shortcomings.

The analogy with power generation comes to the fore once more. We don't leave decision making on whether or not to use nuclear power to nuclear physicists but, after intense public and political debate, decide ourselves, democratically and based on a thorough assessment of the advantages and disadvantages of this form of energy and its alternatives. Even though we do not understand exactly how a nuclear reactor works, we do note the outcomes of this form of energy generation, compare it to other forms, and arrive at a decision.

Actually this analogy applies only partially. When deciding on nuclear energy we give, if we are prudent, significant weight to the opinions of nuclear physicists, engineers, and other energy experts. But unlike economists nuclear scientists have developed adequate knowledge: nuclear power plants work. Economists, as a result of the shortcomings of their science, their distorted picture of reality, theories based less on reality than on faith, and the unrealistic assumptions needed to make their mathematical models work have much less relevant knowledge on the economy.

The above does not mean that, if they manage to put aside those mathematical models and use their intellectual capacities for a thorough analysis of past and present, economists cannot contribute hugely to the discussion. So we should listen, but reject all that which derives from mainstream economic belief and its dogmas. In other words, we should accept and follow up on the opinions of the alleged experts only if it is supported by well-balanced arguments and factual analysis.

An uphill battle

The fight against economic dogma and thus the current economic order is likely to be fiercer than the fight anti-nuclear activists engage in against the nuclear lobby. This is partly because the battle is not fought against engineers and scientists but against the faithful. And also, because economic faith is not only espoused by economists but also by most of our political elite and the media.

Money isn't difficult

Most important is that we should not let ourselves be discouraged by the argument that money and money creation are complex issues that even many experts don't understand well. Because no matter how complicated economists and other financial experts make it, the simple fact is that after all is said and done, money is something very simple, a symbol that works as long as we have faith in it and of which, within limits, we can make as much as we deem necessary. That's the simple but correct starting point of the discussion we must engage in.

Target group: our politicians

That discussion should be sought in particular with those who represent us and are uniquely responsible for the public interest: the political elite. Getting the topic of money creation and our monetary system on the agenda will require broad public support from all those who have in mind both their own interests and those of others: those still suffering from the 2008 crisis, the poor in North and South, those who have no access to proper education and health care, those whose health is suffering under environmental pollution, and above all, future generations.

The transition: planning ahead

The faster the transition to a public monetary system takes place, the better. Realistically speaking, though, it can take a long time before such major change is achieved. It will probably require a new crisis, even worse than the 2008 one – a crisis which according to many experts is close to inevitable.

Maybe we can learn something from the famous economist Milton Friedman, proponent of the Chicago Plan but later in life also a far-right economist with a strong aversion to anything remotely resembling government and state intervention. For several decades Friedman laid the foundations for the policies that were implemented in the early 1980s in the United States and Britain under the Ronald Reagan and Margaret Thatcher administrations. He described the way of bringing about major change as follows: "Only a crisis - actual or perceived - produces real change. When that crisis occurs, the actions that are taken depend on the ideas that are lying around. That, I believe, is our basic function: to develop alternatives to existing policies, to keep them alive and available until the politically impossible becomes the politically inevitable." Friedman wrote this more than twenty years before Reagan and Thatcher brought his ideas into practice.

The lesson we can learn from Friedman is that if the opportunity arises to move from private to public money creation the plans to do so should be ready. For Great Britain and the United States significant efforts have already been made by such organizations as Positive Money and the American Monetary Institute. The plans these organizations developed are probably also applicable for other countries and possibly, monetary unions such as the Eurozone. For each country or group of countries detailed, well worked out plans and draft bills should be prepared and be ready to use. [20]

A role for economists?

As already mentioned there are many economists who are critical of the perspectives, outlook, theory and practice of mainstream economics, and who can think outside the box. That's a good thing because we cannot do without their help. Such economists will be indispensable, in the first instance to overcome the barriers thrown up, consciously or unconsciously, by mainstream economists in defence of banks and the financial industry. And secondly, when that barrier is torn down they will be indispensable in the fight against the interests that draw so much benefit from our present monetary system.

Dutch economist and monetary expert Roelf Haan, an early monetary reformer, sees an especially important role for academic economists, as they can be more independent in their thinking than their fellow economists in government and industry.[21] Haan sees it

---

[20] In 2011 US Congressman Dennis Kucinich of Ohio presented a bill to the US House of Representatives, the "National Emergency Employment Defence (NEED) Act". This proposal, developed with the support of the American Monetary Institute, was based in part on the monetary reform proposed in the 1930s Chicago Plan.

[21] In "*The relationship between the financial sector and the real economy*" (Dutch *De relatie tussen de financiële sector en de reële economie*), 2012, https://docs.google.com/file/d/0B7iNQWnaw2FBUmxXWGdBdVI0bXM/e

as a task for university teachers and researchers to educate the public and policy makers – also when running the risk of their advice being rejected.

Let's hope that academic and other economists accept the challenge of Haan and start contributing to convincing our politicians that reform of our monetary system is not only possible but necessary. Likewise politicians will have to abandon the beaten track. In line with Friedman Haan suggests that politics should be seen not only as the art of the possible but even more so, as the art of making possible tomorrow what seems impossible today.

---

dit, Haan cites from statements from the 1970s by the well-known Belgian-American authority in international monetary economics Robert Triffin, professor at Yale University. It should be noted, however, that since then times have changed: unfortunately, over the past decades academic independence has been compromised increasingly by governments encouraging ever closer links between universities and industry, directly and by forcing public universities to generate more income by working for private enterprise.

POSTSCRIPT: MONEY CREATION AND SUSTAINABLE DEVELOPMENT

Money for sustainable development: a political choice

In the above we discussed why a new financial system is needed and what the alternative, a system in which the state is responsible for money creation, would look like. Also, the different ways were reviewed in which the newly created money is to be channelled into the economy. Distinction was made between expenditures by the state and those by business and citizens. To what extent, that is to say, in what proportions that happens is a political decision that stands apart from the issue of monetary creation. In other words, how to spend the benefits of public money creation is a political choice.

People and groups for which environment, sustainability, social justice and responsibility for future generations are important will plead for spending the benefits mostly on policies contributing to those goals. That implies a major role for government. Others think that citizens and businesses will spend the money more wisely than government, and that the solution of social and environmental problems can best be left to private enterprise and the market. This group will do their utmost to ensure the benefits of money creation end up with citizens and business, through tax cuts and possibly a citizen dividend.

As will be obvious from the main text the author of this booklet belongs to the first group: those who consider that in spending the benefits of public money creation investment in sustainable development should be given priority. This epilogue is in line with that choice. It was separated from the main text because this choice is independent of the need for and benefits of monetary reform as discussed before.

As previously stated, public money creation is indispensable for achieving the goal of an environmentally sustainable, socially just society. Without it governments will not be able to invest in sustainable development on the required scale. On the other hand, public money creation is by no means a guarantee for the realization of such a society. Therefore this epilogue gives special attention to the link between our monetary system and sustainable development.

Attention is also paid to the question of whether in the context of the transition to an ecologically sustainable and socially just society we should aim for stopping economic growth and the transition to a "steady state economy" now. Many groups that deal with environmental issues advocate for such a halt to growth, some advocate economic contraction. An alternative viewpoint is that of "selective growth": instead of an overall increase in the production of all goods and services growth is aimed for only in the production of those goods and services that promote the sustainable use of finite natural resources or otherwise benefit the environment. To this can be added growth in the production and consumption of goods and services that enhance social justice without detrimental effects for the environment. This kind of growth can be referred to as (economic) development rather than (economic) growth.

Money creation and non-sustainable consumption

As already mentioned public money creation would allow for government to use optimally the productive capacity of society to address the environmental and social problems society faces. The investment and jobs required for doing so would also resolve our current economic problems: it would end the economic crisis. From an environmental perspective, however, public money creation is also risky. On the one hand we can argue that the newly created money should be used for investment in sustainability and social justice, but political forces who want to reduce the role of government because they believe businesses and consumers spend money more wisely than government could frustrate those efforts. If they would succeed in having the benefits of public money creation accrue to citizens and businesses rather than to the state the result would be, in today's conditions, a sizeable increase in unsustainable consumption at the expense of the environment and hence, of future generations. The risk of this happening would be considerable as a sizeable reduction in taxes and a citizen's dividend would go down well with a large proportion of the electorate. It would, therefore, be something easy to exploit by politicians.

Unsustainable consumption would increase even if all newly created money were invested in sustainable development. This is because the new jobs, wages and profits resulting from such investments would lead to higher disposable incomes and thereby consumption. As today's consumption is largely unsustainable the proposed change in the monetary system could turn out to work against the much-needed transition to an environmentally sustainable economy.

An integrated approach

To prevent a new monetary system from leading to even more unsustainable production and consumption a comprehensive approach is needed. The new monetary system and investment in sustainable development should be combined with regulation and a "green" tax system which would reward sustainable investment and consumption and discourage unsustainable investment and consumption. For example the use of libraries, theater, public transport and transport by bike can be encouraged by subsidies, and the use of passenger cars using petrol or diesel can be taxed more heavily. At the same time, research should be promoted on cars propelled by (green) electricity, hydrogen or other renewable fuels. The purchase of such cars can be subsidized so the transition from unsustainable to sustainable driving is made as rapidly as possible. In addition, producers would have to be required to produce new cars in as durable a manner as possible, that is, in such a way that raw materials used in production and use are recycled in full.

In other areas also complementary policy will be needed. Government should take the initiative for a series of round table conferences to arrive at agreements, or social contracts, with employers and unions to control prices and wages. Trade agreements would need to ensure that imports and exports would meet minimum standards for environmental and worker protection. Demands on national business regarding maximizing recycling options would also have to apply to imported products, meaning further conditions for trade.

Transition to sustainable: with or without growth?

Many people and organizations advocating a sustainable economy and society advocate transition now, the sooner the better. We must take a step back now. Put an end to growth, and switch to a steady-state economy.

From the perspective of the burden today's economic activity puts on scarce, finite resource that makes sense. But if at this point in time, with the current economic system, we would make the switch towards a zero growth or shrinking economy large numbers of people would remain unemployed, underemployed and poor. Our current economic system is not prepared at all for such a transition because of its addiction to growth and its focus on and bias towards economic activity that generates financial profit. This problem would weigh even heavier on less developed countries, where hundreds of millions of people are still living in extreme poverty and billions more live just above that level.

Proponents of transition now argue that poverty in less developed countries should be solved by the rich nations sharing more: the cake should be distributed more fairly. That's an idea that will find little support in the rich countries, especially among people with lower incomes. And many people with higher incomes too prefer to keep their money for themselves and their families – if only because of the high probability that the transfers to developing countries do not end up with the right people. At present the latter is already often the case with the much smaller transfers of money in the form of development assistance. Moreover economic stagnation or decline in the rich countries would cause, in the current global economic system, major economic damage to developing countries which depend on both domestic growth and growth in exports to developed nations.

First growth, then steady state

An alternative strategy to "stop growth now" is to give a huge but temporary boost to the economy by carrying out a global program for sustainable development. So instead of reducing growth and the transition to steady state there would be more growth – growth coming from the transition to an environmentally sustainable economy and a socially just society. Such a program will not be ecologically sustainable, in the sense that many finite resources will be used in ways that could not be continued for centuries to come. But there would be no need to do so: the program would be a one-off investment which, once completed, could be brought back to the level required for maintenance and gradual replacement. Thus society and the economy would switch gradually to investment and consumption levels at which no more finite resources would be used then could be substituted.

Arriving at a sustainable use of resources would mean reduced investment, which would decrease the amount of work. This decline is likely to occur anyway as a result of technological development, particularly automation. The challenge then becomes to divide the remaining work, which could be achieved by reducing labour hours and job sharing. To ensure that people, despite fewer working hours, would keep an acceptable income a reduction in labour hours could be combined with providing all citizens with a basic income.

Growth for sustainable development

In conclusion, the transition to a society that uses its resources sustainably will have to take place according to the concept of "first-then". First development on such a scale that, because of the associated investment and economic activity, it will not be environmentally sustainable in terms of the use of finite resources; then, when this investment has led to the desired impact, the transition to an environmentally sustainable economy and society.

"First-then" is necessary both for social justice and for implementing the enormous changes that are needed to achieve an ecologically sustainable and socially just society in the shortest possible time. On the fact that there is urgency, in particular as regards climate change, most experts agree. On the other hand, towards the fully or partially unemployed people in rich and poor countries and those in developing countries who subsist on low productive and barely paid work we have a moral obligation to offer sufficiently productive and fairly paid employment and thus, a better life. The better off in the rich nations do not have the right to halt growth as long as those who still need it to improve their living conditions and build a life have not been able to benefit from it. Yet towards future generations we have the obligation to bring about this better life through a different kind of growth: through growth resulting from investments in sustainability and social justice. If as a result of such sustainable growth all basic needs are met – food, water and sanitation, housing, a healthy environment, education, health – and if all environmental issues are adequately addressed the transition to a stationary economy will likewise become a moral imperative.

To summarize: to achieve a socially just and environmentally sustainable society growth will still be needed initially. But it will be a kind of growth that's very different from the growth we have now. It will be growth from investment in sustainable development rather than the drive for profit. As such it will be growth contributing to an ecologically sustainable economy and socially just society rather than growth leading to greater prosperity for the already well-off through more non-sustainable consumption and production.

ANNEX: NETWORKS, READING, VIEWING

In the below links are given to organizations committed to reform of the monetary system and to a number of publications on monetary reform, with a brief description of content.

ORGANISATIONS

Positive Money, http://www.positivemoney.org/, founded in 2010 by Ben Dyson, is the leading British organization for monetary reform. The mission of Positive Money is to change the monetary system in Great Britain in order to achieve a fairer society and a more stable economy. To this purpose Positive Money carries out research, publishes and lobbies British parliament and government. For the short term Positive Money advocates "green quantitative easing": having the Bank of England create money directly for government for investment in the public interest, e.g. energy saving and the generation of renewable energy. The economic activity thus generated would provide an environmentally sustainable way out of the crisis. This would be a good alternative to the current "quantitative easing" which results mainly in newly created money ending up in the speculative economy, laying the basis for the next crisis. The website of Positive Money gives access to a range of relevant publications and videos (see below). Most publications can be downloaded for free as pdfs.

The Positive Money website also contains a page with links to like-minded organizations in other countries: http://internationalmoneyreform.org/member-organisations/.

The New Economics Foundation, NEF, http://www.neweconomics.org is an independent British think tank that was established in 1986 as a result of two international conferences known as TOES (The Other Economic Summit), held parallel to the economic summits of the G8. NEF has developed into a leading British think tank for the promotion of social, economic and environmental justice. The purpose of NEF is to bring about a transition ("The Great Transition") to a new economy that works for society and planet. In support of this NEF carries out research, puts into practice the ideas developed, and cooperates with like-minded organizations, nationally and internationally, to bring about change.

The website Sovereign Money, http://sovereignmoney.eu/, launched by the German economic sociologist Joseph Huber, with close ties to NEF.

The American Monetary Institute, http://www.monetary.org/, founded in 1996, is the largest US organization in the field of monetary reform. AMI holds annual conferences and works closely with among others congressman Dennis Kucinich of Ohio. In 2011 Kucinich presented a bill that included monetary reform to the US House of Representatives. This National Emergency Employment Defense (NEED) Act, co-developed with AMI, contains an adapted version of the 1930s' Chicago Plan. AMI strongly advocates spending the benefits of public money creation through government investment in ("eco-friendly") infrastructure, healthcare and education.

The Public Banking Insitute, http://PublicBankingInstitute.org, was established in 2010 by American lawyer Ellen Brown as a result of her research, initiated in 2008, into alternatives to the banking that caused the 2008 crisis. Her research led her to the conclusion that the best option is public money creation, and to the only state-owned bank in the United States: the Bank of North Dakota, with an excellent track record that goes back 90 years.

VIDEOS

Why is there so much debt? (https://www.youtube.com/watch?v=lrQX4CF6Bxs)

An excellent 3-minute video on Youtube from Positive Money, on the unsustainable indebtedness inherent to the current monetary system and the need for a new system based on public money creation. Should be required viewing for all politicians and economists – and is a must for all those who feel concerned by the fate of society and humanity. The Youtube page with this video also has, in the column on the right, suggestions for a range of other interesting videos.

http://www.publicbankinginstitute.org/victoria_grant. A twelve year old Canadian girl explains in less than seven minutes how the Canadian citizenry is being exploited by the existing monetary system and how things can be done differently: by having parliament choose for public money creation.

More videos on http://www.positivemoney.org/videos/ and http://www.publicbankinginstitute.org/videos. On the Positive Money page among others a link to the independent documentary 97% Owned. This documentary of 130 minutes shows, through interviews with economists, politicians, former bankers and activists, how the debt-based privatized monetary system leads to one crisis after another and pushes up housing prices.

BOOKS AND REPORTS

Modernising Money, Andrew Jackson & Ben Dyson, Positive Money, Londen 2013.

https://www.positivemoney.org/modernising-money/; a summary can be downloaded for free from http://www.positivemoney.org/wp-content/uploads/2013/01/Modernising-Money-Free-Overview.pdf

This book provides a detailed description of the ins and outs of the transition of the British monetary system from private to public. The book begins with a brief history of money and continues with a description of the current monetary system and its economic, social and ecological impact on the economy and society. The need for growth inherent in linking money creation to debt and thereby to the need to pay interest leads to the pursuit of short-term profit rather than long-term public goals. This leads to the unsustainable exploitation of resources and activities which, though profitable in the short run, have no social utility or run counter to the public interest. The book points out that the current monetary system puts enormous power in the hands of a small group of people with neither responsibility for nor accountability towards society.

The second part of the book shows how the privilege of creating money can be taken away from private banks which from then on will work only work with already created money. This can be achieved by placing the responsibility of creating money with a

Monetary Creation Committee. Newly created money will be channelled into the economy in various ways: through government spending, direct payments to citizens, repayment of public debt, and lending through the existing banking system.

The book lists the benefits of the proposed reform: it will end financial crises caused by speculation, increase government revenues, decrease debt and hence debt obligations, and ensure a stable money supply. The need to grow disappears and much more room is created for investment in the environment and social services. Money creation is transparent and the impact of the financial sector on society and politics decreases. Banks are no longer "too big to fail", meaning they need not be saved but can fail if they do not function properly. The book argues the reforms can be instituted in the UK alone without weakening the British pound: the greater risk is an increase in value.

Sovereign Money, Paving the way for a sustainable recovery. Positive Money. http://www.positivemoney.org/wp-content/uploads/2013/11/Sovereign-Money-Final-Web.pdf

Freely downloadable report with a proposal for "Sovereign Money Creation" (SMC): creation of money by the (British) central bank, to be provided directly to the government for public investment, tax cuts and possibly a lump sum payment to citizens: a "citizens' dividend". The report focuses not so much on a complete transformation of the financial system as on the creation of a tool, SMC, that can lead to a sustainable recovery of the economy rather than, as presently, a temporary recovery based on even more debt. In the longer term SMC can avoid economic stagnation and contraction by providing government with the means to ensure sufficient demand for goods and services. The report shows in detail how SMC can be put into practice and clearly describes the steps to be taken and the benefits and foreseeable effects. It also discusses the risk of abuse by politicians and how this can be prevented: by putting the decision making on the amount of money to be created with a central bank monetary committee operating independently of government and parliament. Government and parliament decide on how the money is spent but are required to submit a spending plan to the Committee prior to the creation of the amount involved. Thus money creation and decision-making on spending are strictly separated. The report indicates that a similar approach has been proposed by leading economists such as John Maynard Keynes and Milton Friedman, and that the UK Treasury too has indicated that it is possible for the financial authorities to finance government deficits through money creation. The report also quotes former British central bank governor Adair Turner, who in a speech in 2013 referred to the taboo in economic circles on the idea of public money creation for financing government spending.

Creating a Sovereign Monetary System. Positive Money, 2014.
http://2joz611prdme3eogq61h5p3gr08.wpengine.netdna-cdn.com/wp-content/uploads/2014/07/Creating_a_Sovereign_Monetary_System_Web20130615.pdf

Freely downloadable report with a detailed proposal for monetary reform: the transition to a "sovereign monetary system" in which the right to money creation is reserved exclusively for the state, and banks can no longer create money through lending. The report is largely based on the above described book *Modernising Money*.

Creating New Money, Joseph Huber and James Robertson, 2000. New Economics Foundation; http://www.neweconomics.org/publications/entry/creating-new-money

This book / report by NEF (free download), dating back to well before the 2008 financial crisis, discusses extensively the different aspects of what the authors call "seignoriage reform". Seignoriage refers to the right to create money and collect the benefits of using that right. The book describes the importance and benefits of taking away the right to create money from private banks and allocate it to a public institution, the central bank, so that the benefits of seigniorage accrue to society as a whole. New, debt free money would be put into circulation through government spending, and not as presently through lending by commercial banks. The book indicates the steps in the reform process and the roles of different agencies, and discusses what countries might undertake it. It also indicates who wins and who would lose: both the economic, social and environmental benefits are described and the advantages for public finance, households and businesses.

The Chicago Plan Revisited - Jaromir Benes and Michael Kumhof. IMF Working Paper WP/12/202

http://www.imf.org/external/pubs/ft/wp/2012/wp12202.pdf

This publication of the International Monetary Fund (IMF), cited a few times in the main text of this booklet, "tests" the plan for public money creation from the 1930s: the "Chicago Plan", named after the university of its most well-known proponents. The plan proposes the transfer of the responsibility for money creation from private banks to government. The functions of money creation and credit supply, in the 1930s as well as today both reserved for private banks, would thus be separated. At the time the proposal was supported by a large group of economists, including some of the most prominent of the period. The plan almost made it into law and was close to implementation under the Roosevelt administration, but in the end the bank lobby prevailed and managed to block the legislation.

For lay persons the more interesting part of the publication is not so much the mathematical modelling with which the assumptions about the benefits of the plan are tested but the brief description of the history of money, of different financial systems, and of advantages and disadvantages of those systems. The analysis shows that systems based on money creation by private banks have led to frequent smaller and larger crises and periods of hyperinflation. The notorious German hyperinflation of the 1920s was the result primarily of speculation by private banks, with support of a central bank that had been privatized shortly before, under pressure from the Allied winners of the First World War.

The report also describes how through the centuries public money creation has been the rule rather than the exception, and has worked well in most cases. It also gives pointers on how to ensure the latter: 1) Do not have the money system managed by a convicted felon, such as John Law in France from 1717 to 1720, and 2) Don't start a war, or when you do make sure you win it. The following summary is given: *"To summarize, the Great Depression was just the latest historical episode to suggest that privately controlled money creation has much more problematic consequences than government money creation. Many leading economists of the time were aware of this historical fact. They also clearly understood the specific problems of bank-based money creation, including the fact that high and potentially destabilizing debt levels become necessary just to create a sufficient money supply, and the fact that banks and their fickle optimism about business conditions effectively control broad monetary aggregates. The formulation of the Chicago Plan was the logical consequence of these insights.*" The report indicates as the main problem of private banking that in good times too much money is created, leading to speculative bubbles and crises, whereas in bad times too little money is created as banks curtail their lending just when it is most needed to help the economy recover. The non-technical sections of this report are a "Must read" for all economists, politicians and journalists dealing with economic and financial issues.

MORE TECHNICAL PUBLICATIONS

Money creation in the modern economy. Michael McLeay, Amar Radia and Ryland Thomas, Bank of England (2014).

http://www.bankofengland.co.uk/publications/Documents/quarterlybulletin/2014/qb14q102.pdf

This paper by the Bank of England explains how in modern economies money is created by commercial banks when they extend a loan. It thus dispels the popular misconception that banks act only as intermediaries, by lending out savings and money provided by the central bank. The paper indicates that ultimately the amount of money entering the economy depends on the monetary policy of the central bank, with as tools interest rates and quantitative easing.

Where does money come from? Tony Greenham & Josh Ryan-Collins, New Economics Foundation, 2012.

http://www.neweconomics.org/publications/entry/where-does-money-come-from

In line with the title this book provides a detailed description of the workings of our current money system, in particular the fact that the money supply is determined mainly by the demand for credit. The book gives an overview of the history of money and banking, describes the current system, the regulation of money creation and distribution, and public finance and foreign currency. The conclusions contain recommendations for further regulation and reform.

Full Reserve Banking. An analysis of four monetary reform plans. Study for the Sustainable Finance Lab, Charlotte van Dixhoorn, 2013.

http://sustainablefinancelab.nl/files/2013/07/Full-Reserve-Banking-Dixhoorn-SFL.pdf

This report contains the findings of a research project on monetary reform commissioned by the Sustainable Finance Lab of the University of Utrecht, The Netherlands. The report is based on interviews with both supporters and opponents of monetary reform. The study summarizes and compares four proposals for monetary reform, including the Chicago Plan and that of Positive Money. The study concludes that it is doubtful whether public money creation as proposed by Positive Money will really have the intended effects and benefits, and mentions there are risks and disadvantages. However, this conclusion is not substantiated whereas the drawbacks of the current system are barely discussed.

Unfortunately the report, which doubles as an MSc thesis, does not provide information on how the conclusions of the report were arrived at. Apparently they are a kind of summary, a middle road between the wide range of opinions expressed by the interviewed experts. Since this group includes many established economists the critical attitude towards monetary reform and the call for more research ("full reserve banking is a valuable research topic in an attempt to find a new structure for our monetary system") comes as no surprise. It may be concluded that the overrepresentation of conventionally thinking economists among the respondents has, unfortunately, led to a poorly justified questioning of the benefits of monetary reform. Especially the critique of the monetary reform approach of Positive Money is not substantiated. Perhaps an inevitable outcome, given the design of the study and the methodology chosen. The study is added to this list of publications because of its comparison of different monetary reform systems and because it illustrates well the obstacles to monetary reform posed by mainstream economics and its practitioners.